BODY NEEDS

Carbohydrates
for a Healthy Body

Hazel King

Heinemann
LIBRARY

www.heinemann.co.uk/library

Visit our website to find out more information about **Heinemann Library** books.

To order:
- ☎ Phone 44 (0) 1865 888066
- 🖹 Send a fax to 44 (0) 1865 314091
- 🖥 Visit the Heinemann Bookshop at www.heinemann.co.uk/library to browse our catalogue and order online.

Heinemann Library is an imprint of Capstone Global Library Limited, a company incorporated in England and Wales having its registered office at 7 Pilgrim Street, London, EC4V 6LB – Registered company number: 6695582

"Heinemann" is a registered trademark of Pearson Education Limited, under licence to Capstone Global Library Limited

Text © Capstone Global Library Limited 2003, 2009
Second edition first published in hardback in 2009
Second edition first published in paperback in 2009
The moral rights of the proprietor have been asserted.

Edited by Louise Galpine, Catherine Clarke, and Claire Throp
Designed by Victoria Bevan and AMR Design Ltd
Original illustrations © Capstone Global Library Ltd
Illustrations by Geoff Ward and p.41 by BigTop
Picture research by Mica Brancic
Originated by Steve Walker
Printed and bound in China by CTPS

ISBN 978 0 431 16724 4 (hardback)
13 12 11 10 09
10 9 8 7 6 5 4 3 2 1

ISBN 978 0 431 16730 5 (paperback)
13 12 11 10 09
10 9 8 7 6 5 4 3 2 1

British Library Cataloguing in Publication Data
King, Hazel
Carbohydrates. – 2nd edition – (Body needs)
613.2'83
A full catalogue record for this book is available from the British Library.

Acknowledgements

We would like to thank the following for allowing their pictures to be reproduced in this publication: ©Action plus: p. **33**; ©Gareth Boden: pp. **8, 11, 12, 17, 21, 23, 34, 35, 42**; ©Getty/FPG: p. **40**; ©Gettyone Stone: p. **24**; ©Liz Eddison: pp. **6, 7, 9, 13, 20, 28, 38, 43**; ©Photolibrary Group Ltd: pp. **29** (Foodpix/Kurt Wilson), **30** (Foodpix/Brian Hagiwara), **31** (Fresh Food Images/Hilary Moore), **37** (Corbis); ©Robert Harrison: p. **4**; ©SPL/Quest: p. **16**; ©Trevor Clifford: p. **36**; ©Tudor Photography: p. **5**; ©Zefa: p. **39**.

Cover photograph of green, red, and white ribbon pasta reproduced with permission of ©PhotoLibrary Group/Food Collection.

The author would like to thank Thomas King and Frank Reakes for their stories.

We would like to thank Dr Sarah Schenker for her invaluable assistance in the preparation of this book.

Contents

Why do we need to eat?	**4**
What are carbohydrates?	**6**
Sugars and starches	**8**
Complicated fibre	**10**
Energy efficient	**12**
Digesting carbohydrates	**14**
Absorbing carbohydrates	**16**
Energy release	**18**
Energy and exercise	**20**
Dental health	**22**
Too much of a good thing	**24**
Staying healthy	**26**
Labelling sugar	**28**
Food labels	**30**
Sugar control	**32**
Food allergies	**34**
Staple starches	**36**
Worldwide diets	**38**
Eating for health	**40**
Achieving a balance	**42**
Glossary	**44**
Find out more	**47**
Index	**48**

Any words appearing in the text in bold, **like this**, are explained in the glossary.

Why do we need to eat?

Eating can be great fun, especially midnight snacks or special treats, but have you ever stopped to wonder why we eat? Food is not there just for our pleasure; it is also needed to keep us alive and healthy.

Nutrients

All foods and drinks provide **energy** and **nutrients**. The main nutrients are carbohydrates, **fats,** and **proteins**. Nutrients are needed to provide energy and help your body grow and repair itself. This book is about carbohydrates, what they are, and how the body uses them. You will need to find out about the other nutrients that your body needs to be healthy. Most foods provide a mixture of different types of nutrients but some provide more of one type of nutrient than another. Your body needs nutrients every day; this is why you have to eat food. In addition, you must drink water, which, although not a nutrient, is essential for health.

Important roles

Each nutrient has an important job to do in the body. For example, you may know that carbohydrates provide the body with energy. Carbohydrates are provided by foods like bread, pasta, rice, sugar, and potatoes. Fats also provide energy. Foods like butter, oil, or margarine contain fats and a small amount of them can provide a lot of energy. Protein is provided by foods like meat, fish, eggs, nuts, and lentils. Protein is needed to help make new **cells** throughout the body.

Without the energy that food provides, leading a healthy, active life would not be possible.

This diagram explains the different nutrients and their role in the body. Only some of the **vitamins** and **minerals** your body needs are shown.

CARBOHYDRATES provide your body with the energy it needs physically (to move about) and internally (breathing, heart beating, brain working).

B VITAMINS help to release energy from food.

VITAMIN A helps eyesight and growth of the skin.

WATER makes up a large proportion of the body. It transports substances and allows **chemical reactions** to take place in the body.

CALCIUM helps to make strong bones and teeth.

VITAMIN E helps keep the body healthy.

VITAMIN C helps to keep skin and gums healthy.

FATS provide vitamins A, D, E, and K, help to keep us warm, and supply energy if it is not supplied by carbohydrate foods.

VITAMIN D works with calcium to build strong bones and teeth.

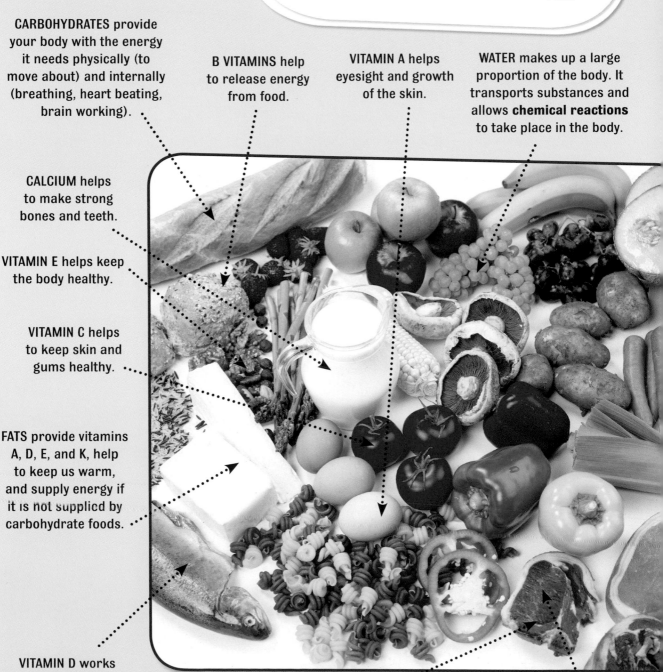

IRON is important for giving blood cells their red colour.

PROTEIN is needed to make new cells and repair any damaged ones. Protein is the main substance found in muscles, skin, and internal **organs**.

What are carbohydrates?

There are three types of carbohydrate found in the diet: sugar, starch, and **fibre**.

Sugars

Sugars are sometimes called "simple carbohydrates" because they are made up of small numbers of **molecules**. A molecule is a very small part of a substance. Molecules of sugar are very small so are absorbed into our bloodstream very easily when we eat foods that contain sugar. Sugars can be found in foods such as fruits, honey, and even milk. These foods contain **natural sugars**. Sugars also come in a variety of forms, such as caster sugar, icing sugar, and demerara sugar. These are added to other foods, for example, to biscuits. All types of sugar provide your body with energy.

Starches

Starches are more complicated than sugars so they take longer for your body to **digest**. During digestion all foods are broken down into molecules. When starches are broken down, they end up as molecules of **glucose**. Glucose is a sugar. This means that starches are actually made up of lots of glucose molecules joined together, so they also provide your body with energy. Foods containing starches include potatoes, rice, pasta, bread, couscous, and polenta.

Carbohydrates can be found in a wide variety of foods.

Fibre

Fibre is the most complicated carbohydrate. Unlike sugar and starch, fibre does not provide you with energy but it does have an important role to play during the digestion of food. Foods that provide lots of fibre include any **wholemeal** or wholewheat products, such as bread, brown rice, pasta, and some breakfast cereals. All fruits and vegetables, pulses (peas, beans, and lentils), oats, barley, and nuts will provide some fibre.

CHOOSING FOOD

Today, most people can choose from a wide variety of foods. Lots of different foods are available, including ready-meals and take-aways.

What is the carbohydrate in my food?

Food	Source of carbohydrate
pizza	pizza base
curry and rice	rice and any vegetables
spaghetti bolognese	spaghetti
beans on toast	beans and bread
lemonade/cola	sugar

All the foods in this meal of pasta and vegetables, garlic bread, milk, and fruit contain carbohydrates.

Sugars and starches

Sugars

Many people say they have a "sweet tooth" because they enjoy the taste of sweet foods. In Britain, foods have been sweetened for centuries. Honey was used by the Romans to add sweetness and to make drinks such as **mead**. Today there is a huge range of different sugars available to use in food preparation.

golden syrup

caster sugar

granulated sugar

maple syrup

sugar cubes

icing sugar

demerara sugar

honey

sugar crystals

muscavado sugar

Sugar comes in many different forms.

The role of sugars

Sugars can be very useful when preparing foods. Sugars are sweet so they are often added to savoury foods, such as tomato sauce, to make them more appealing. Sugars can be used to add colour to foods, either by using brown sugar or because when sugars are cooked they turn a golden-brown colour. Sugars are used to **preserve** some foods, such as jam, and are used to make food look attractive when used as icing or decoration.

Starches

Starches are used very differently from sugars in the preparation of food. First of all, starches are not sweet. In fact, on its own a starch is quite bland – imagine eating raw flour! Most starchy foods have other ingredients added to them when meals are made. For example, pasta is served with a sauce, baked potatoes have a filling added, and bread is made into sandwiches or toast.

Starches are still very useful when preparing food. Starches are able to thicken liquids. If potatoes are added to casseroles, the sauce will become less runny. Cornflour is another example of a starch being used to thicken foods. It can be used to thicken liquids or sauces and is also added to custard powder to help make custard.

Starches absorb (take in) liquids so, when rice or potatoes are cooked in a saucepan of water, they become soft because of the water they absorb.

Starch facts

When starchy foods are eaten they are broken down into simple sugars (glucose). If you chew a piece of bread for a few minutes you will find it eventually tastes sweet. This is because the starch is being broken down by the saliva in your mouth.

These starch-rich potatoes are being cooked in a saucepan by simmering them in water. The hard, raw potatoes absorb water during cooking and become soft.

Complicated fibre

Fibre is often referred to as the **complex carbohydrate** because it has a complicated structure. The human **digestive system** is unable to break it down so the body does not get any nutrients from fibre. But, the fibre is important because it helps the body's digestion. Fibre helps to make waste products soft and easy to pass out of your body. You will find out more about the digestive system on pages 14 and 15.

Insoluble fibre

There are two types of fibre: **insoluble fibre** and **soluble fibre**. The first is found in **bran** and products containing bran. Foods like wholemeal bread are made from wheat, which contains bran. It is known as insoluble fibre because it cannot **dissolve** in a liquid such as water.

Wholemeal or wholewheat products are sometimes called "unrefined" foods. Wheat, for example, can be **processed** so that most of the outer bran is removed and the flour that is produced is white in colour. This type of flour provides some fibre. But if all the wheat grain is used (including the bran and **germ**) the flour that results contains a lot more fibre, which is helpful for your digestive system. Products made with this type of flour are less "refined". Insoluble fibre passes through the body without changing very much at all. It can soak up liquids inside your body, and helps food move through your digestive system easily.

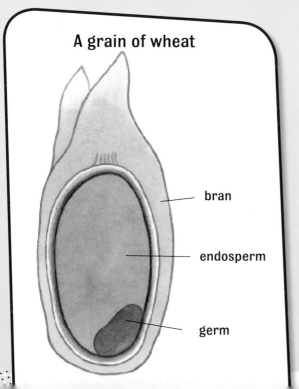

A grain of wheat

bran

endosperm

germ

FIBRE AND COOKING

When using ingredients that contain fibre you have to remember that they will act a bit differently. For example, if you make bread or pastry using wholemeal flour you must add extra liquid because the bran will soak up more liquid than white flour. Foods made with wholemeal or wholewheat flour will also tend to become dry more quickly than products made using white flour.

Oats are a good source of soluble fibre, so eating porridge for breakfast is a great start to the day!

Soluble fibre

Soluble fibre is found in foods like oats, vegetables, and fruit. By including plenty of fruit and vegetables in your diet you keep your digestive system healthy. You will also benefit from the various vitamins and minerals that the fruit and vegetables provide.

Soluble fibre can help lower blood **cholesterol** levels. Soluble fibre in the diet can bind to bile **acids**, which are released into the gut to aid the digestion of fat in the diet. The binding of bile acids to soluble fibre means that they are not able to be reabsorbed by the body to be used again. This means the body needs to make more bile acids, and this process uses up cholesterol, so helping to lower levels in the blood.

Energy efficient

You need energy

Carbohydrates are an excellent source of energy. Energy is needed so your body can grow, repair itself, and keep warm. Even when you are asleep your body needs energy in order to function properly. Without energy you would not survive. You need it to breathe, digest food, and even think! In fact, it is your brain that is the most energy-demanding organ in your body.

Every cell in your body needs the sugar called glucose and it is particularly important to your **nervous system**, red blood cells, and brain. Glucose is the sugar that carbohydrates are broken down into when they are digested. After eating foods containing carbohydrates, some of the energy will be used straight away while the rest of it will be stored.

Glycogen stores

Any glucose that is not immediately needed by the body is stored in the **liver** or stays in the muscles. However, it is not stored as glucose. Instead it is converted into a substance known as **glycogen**. Carbohydrates are such a good source of energy because glycogen is quickly and easily turned back into glucose as soon as it is needed.

Measuring energy

The energy that is released from food is measured in **kilojoules (kJ)**. Today this unit is usually used in schools and by **nutritionists** or **dieticians**, but food labels often still show energy values as **calories**. People can look at food labels to see how much energy will be provided by a meal or product.

The human body uses 252 kJ every hour just to sleep!

Energy from food

All foods and most drinks provide energy. Water is one drink that does not supply any kilojoules. The amount of energy supplied by a food depends on what the food contains. Foods that are high in fats will have a high energy value because fat provides the most kilojoules.

There are typically 4 calories per gram of carbohydrate. For example, a slice of bread has 15 grams of carbohydrate, which makes 60 calories from carbohydrate (15 grams x 4 calories = 60 calories). Fat has 9 calories per gram and protein 4 calories per gram.

CARBOHYDRATES AND FATS

It is interesting to compare the number of kilojoules that carbohydrate foods supply on their own and when combined with fats. For example, 100 grams of boiled potatoes provide 330 kilojoules. But when potatoes are made into chips (which means they are fried in oil) the energy values rise dramatically to 796 kilojoules.

All foods provide energy, but different foods supply energy in different amounts of kilojoules. Butter is higher in energy value than meat or bagels.

Digesting carbohydrates

Carbohydrates may be a good source of energy but, until they have been broken down, your body cannot use the energy. The process of breaking down food is called digestion. After food has been digested it must be absorbed in a form that can be used by your body.

Chew it

The first stage of digestion takes place in your mouth. You physically start breaking down the food with your teeth by biting and chewing it. At the same time chemicals called **enzymes** in your saliva start attacking the starch. Enzymes are chemicals that speed up the breakdown of food. Large molecules in food are broken down into smaller ones. The saliva also makes the food moist and easier to swallow.

Swallow it

The moist, chewed-up food is then swallowed and passes down a long tube called the **oesophagus** (see diagram). At the end of the oesophagus is the stomach, which is like a stretchy bag. Carbohydrate foods stay in the stomach for about two to three hours while being churned around and made into a mushy liquid called **chyme**. **Digestive juices** containing enzymes continue to attack the food and break it down.

Absorb it

The chyme gradually passes from the stomach into the **small intestine**, where further breakdown takes place. By now the food consists of tiny molecules, which are small enough to pass through the walls of the small intestine into the bloodstream (see diagram). You will find out more about absorption on pages 16 and 17.

Move it

You will see from the diagram that the digestive system is very long. Food cannot pass along it by itself – it needs some help. This help comes from the muscles in the walls of the intestines, which squeeze and relax, pushing the food along.

Release it

Any food that is not useful to the body will not be absorbed into the blood. Instead, it will pass from the small intestine into the **large intestine**. This is where any insoluble fibre will end up. As the remaining food particles travel along the large intestine, water is absorbed back into the body. Finally, waste matter is released from the body through the anus when you go to the toilet.

Food facts

Food can take at least 24 hours to travel through the intestines. When the intestines are stretched out, they are about as long as a double-decker bus!

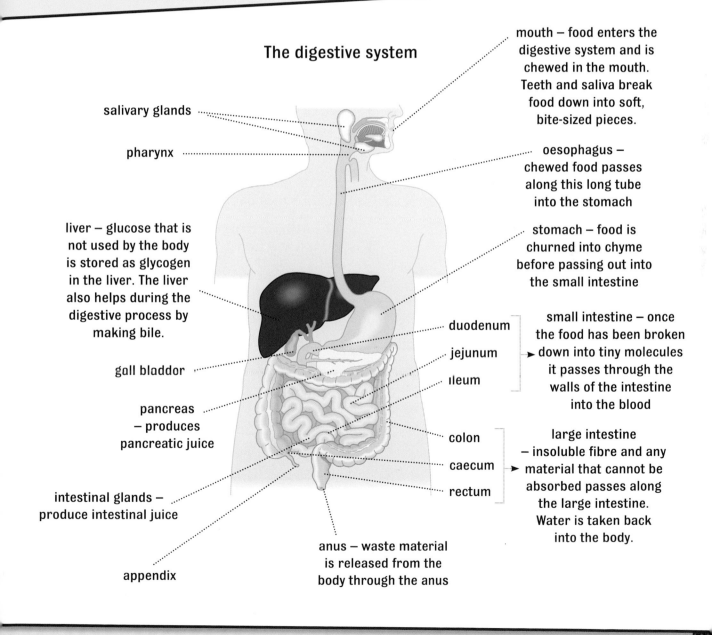

The digestive system

salivary glands

pharynx

liver – glucose that is not used by the body is stored as glycogen in the liver. The liver also helps during the digestive process by making bile.

gall bladder

pancreas – produces pancreatic juice

intestinal glands – produce intestinal juice

appendix

mouth – food enters the digestive system and is chewed in the mouth. Teeth and saliva break food down into soft, bite-sized pieces.

oesophagus – chewed food passes along this long tube into the stomach

stomach – food is churned into chyme before passing out into the small intestine

duodenum

jejunum

ileum

small intestine – once the food has been broken down into tiny molecules it passes through the walls of the intestine into the blood

colon

caecum

rectum

large intestine – insoluble fibre and any material that cannot be absorbed passes along the large intestine. Water is taken back into the body.

anus – waste material is released from the body through the anus

Absorbing carbohydrates

The nutrients in the food that you eat need to get to all the cells in your body. There would be no point eating and digesting food unless your body had some way of getting the food into your bloodstream and transporting it around the body. The process that your body uses to do this is called absorption. This takes place in the small intestine.

Small intestine

By the time you are fully grown your small intestine is about 7 metres (23 feet) long. It is made up of three parts: the **duodenum**, the **jejunum**, and the **ileum**. Carbohydrates and proteins are absorbed in the jejunum, but fats are absorbed in the ileum. The small intestine looks like a folded tube that joins your stomach and your large intestine.

Tiny villi

The inside lining of the small intestine is covered with millions of tiny hair-like projections called **villi**. Each villus is about half a millimetre long and has even smaller "microvilli" covering it! This is a very clever way to increase the surface area of the small intestine. Surface area is the space occupied by the surface of something.

Molecules of digested food pass through the walls of the villi and into the blood vessels. It is important that all the food molecules are absorbed into your bloodstream so you can benefit from the nutrients. To do this, there must be as much surface area as possible to allow all the molecules to pass through the cell walls.

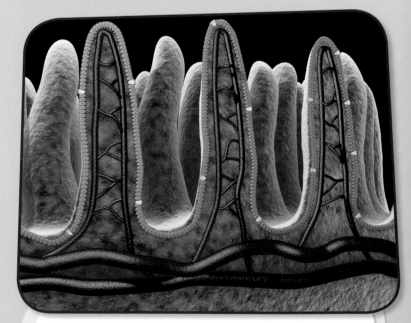

The lining of the small intestine is covered with villi, and the villi are covered with microvilli. Here you can see microvilli from the small intestine.

Molecules of food

When carbohydrate foods are broken down, the tiny glucose molecules are absorbed through the walls of the small intestine and into the blood. The blood transports the molecules to the liver for processing. The food molecules include glucose from the breakdown of carbohydrates, **amino acids** from the breakdown of protein, and **fatty acids** from the breakdown of fats.

Leftover matter

Any food that remains after the absorption process has to be removed from the body. This sludgy matter contains the fibre that helps to keep the waste soft and bulky. This means it can leave the body more easily.

Body fact

It may be surprising to learn that much of your body is made up of water. There is water in your blood, saliva, urine, and in all the cells of your body, including your bones, muscles, and skin. As you can lose as much as 3 litres (6 pints) of water every day in your sweat, urine, and breath, it is important to replace that moisture.

Your body gets water from the foods you eat and liquids you drink. Without water, the body would not be able to absorb nutrients from food.

Energy release

Food for fuel

Your body needs fuel to provide you with energy in the same way a car needs petrol or diesel to make it go. Carbohydrate foods are the best type of "fuel" for your body because they are broken down into glucose, which can be used by every cell in your body.

Your bloodstream is a bit like a car's petrol tank. It needs to have a constant level of glucose in the blood so cells can use it whenever energy is needed. If there is more than your body needs, the liver changes the extra glucose into glycogen and stores it. The liver also changes the glycogen back into glucose as soon as the glucose energy in the blood is used up.

Turning food into fuel

The process of turning food into energy is a complicated one. Every cell in your body has a tiny "energy factory" where a series of chemical reactions happen. The result is the release of energy. **Oxygen** is needed for this to happen properly. During this process **carbon dioxide** and water are produced. There is carbon dioxide in our breath when we breathe out. The amount of energy you need depends on your weight, age, whether you are a boy or a girl, and the type and amount of activity you are doing. Children and teenagers require a lot of energy compared to their size because their bodies are still growing. Boys tend to need more energy than girls and girls tend to have more body fat than boys. Different activities need different amounts of energy; running requires more energy than walking, but walking requires more than sitting. The weather can also affect your energy levels. If the weather is cold your body will have to work hard trying to keep you warm.

Be active!

People who are inactive are more prone to weight gain than those who lead active lifestyles. It is recommended that children and young people aim to do at least an hour of physical activity every day, and that adults aim to do at least 30 minutes of physical activity five days a week.

Constant levels

The best foods for keeping your **blood sugar levels** constant are those that contain complex carbohydrates. This is because they are gradually broken down and release their sugar slowly into the bloodstream. Wholegrain foods, beans, fruit, and some vegetables are all slow-release carbohydrate foods. Sweets, on the other hand, cause blood sugar levels to rise quickly. This in turn makes the body try to lower the level. Blood sugar levels fall again creating a feeling of hunger. If more sweets are eaten the whole process starts again.

This diagram shows how energy is released from food when we eat.

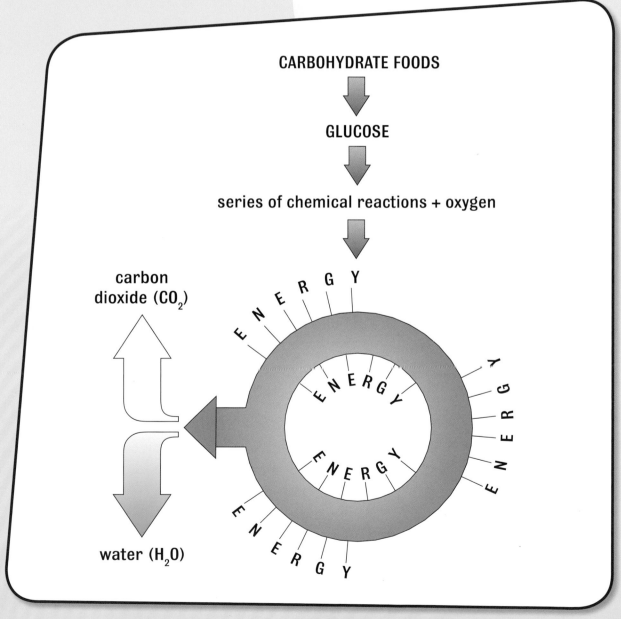

CARBOHYDRATE FOODS

GLUCOSE

series of chemical reactions + oxygen

carbon dioxide (CO$_2$)

ENERGY

ENERGY

ENERGY

ENERGY

ENERGY

water (H$_2$O)

Energy and exercise

The amount of energy you need just to maintain your body, while you are doing absolutely nothing, is known as the **basal metabolic rate (BMR)**. The rate depends on the amount of muscle in the body. This means it will vary according to your weight, age, and whether you are a boy or a girl. Boys usually require more kilojoules than girls per day and the difference increases as children get older.

In and out

The energy your body receives from food is known as its energy input. The amount of energy it uses is its output. Ideally, the input and output should be roughly the same. However, if your energy input is higher than your output your body will store any extra as fat and you may put on weight. On the other hand, if your input is lower than your output you may lose weight. A good diet is one that ensures you stay at a healthy weight.

Nutritionists recommend that most of your energy should be provided by carbohydrate foods.

Energy you might need during various activities

Activity	Energy needed for one hour
running	2419 kJ
swimming	1612 kJ
walking	1083 kJ
sleeping	256 kJ

Of course, you cannot work out how much energy you are going to use each day and then eat the right amount of food! Usually people rely on what their body is telling them and eat if they feel hungry and stop when they feel full. However, sometimes it is important to plan ahead, especially if you know you are going to do a lot of exercise. If, for example, you are going to do a lot of running you would know to fuel your body by eating meals containing pasta a few days beforehand.

Body fact

When running a **marathon**, your body starts off using blood sugar (glucose) then it uses glycogen stores. When glycogen runs out, and if no other energy is supplied, the body breaks down fat or protein to make its energy. However, this is much more effort for the body.

TOM'S STORY

Tom King uses plenty of energy doing various sports every week, including tennis, golf, cricket, and swimming. However, his favourite sport is football. He plays forward for the California Boys in the East Berkshire League. He knows how to keep up his energy levels and stay healthy. Tom says: "I normally eat things like carrots, cucumber, and lots of pasta. I have beans on toast before a big match and I only have crisps and fizzy drinks on special occasions — or when my mum lets me!"

When you eat pasta, the energy that your body receives from it is released slowly.

Dental health

Today's healthy-eating advice tells us to reduce the amount of sugar we eat. If you often eat sugary foods your teeth can become damaged. Sugars left in the mouth attract **bacteria** that multiply resulting in the production of acid. Acid conditions cause tooth enamel to break down and teeth become damaged. This is known as dental caries ("caries" means "rotten").

Brush well

After eating sugary foods your saliva helps the mouth to return to normal but this takes about thirty minutes. For this reason, if you do eat sweets, it is better to eat them all in one go rather than a few at a time. It is also better for your teeth if you choose sweets that can be eaten quickly. Sweets that are sucked give bacteria the conditions they enjoy for longer so they are likely to cause more damage. Of course, if you can, you should clean your teeth after eating any foods, especially sticky ones. Teeth should be brushed twice a day using a **fluoride** toothpaste.

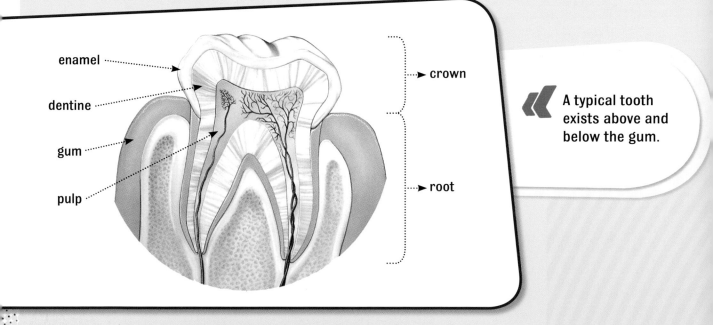

enamel

dentine

gum

pulp

crown

root

A typical tooth exists above and below the gum.

Inside, outside

Sugars can be divided into two categories: those found inside food cells and those that are not. The first type includes glucose, produced when carbohydrates are broken down, and fructose, which is found in some fruits. The second type includes the sugars used during baking (such as caster sugar, soft brown sugar, and demerara sugar) and also honey.

Health experts agree that a healthy diet should include only a small amount of foods containing fructose, the second type of sugar. This is because these sugars are found mainly in foods like cakes, biscuits, sweets, puddings, fizzy drinks, and many ready-made meals. These foods tend to be high in sugars (as well as fats) and contain few complex carbohydrates.

Sweet treats

Although sugar provides your body with energy it does not provide any nutrients. Sugar does not contain vitamins, minerals, protein, starches, fibre, or fats. This is another reason why health experts believe it is better to get energy from foods that also provide us with vitamins or other nutrients. When you are hungry it is better to choose fruit or a sandwich instead of sweets. You will gain more vitamins and minerals and it will be better for your teeth!

It is fine to eat sweets as a treat every now and then but always clean your teeth afterwards.

Too much of a good thing

Food is the fuel you need to give you energy, but food can also be fun! Other animals do not treat food in the same way that humans do. Animals tend to eat when they are hungry and only eat the food their body needs. People spend much more time thinking about food. They shop for, prepare, cook, and serve food. They can choose to eat at a restaurant or order meals from a take-away. Unlike animals, we have a great deal of choice when it comes to food.

 Fast foods may be tasty but they are often high in fat.

More carbohydrate, less fat

Everyone is being encouraged to include plenty of complex carbohydrate foods in their diet. But the trouble with many of today's meals is that they also include lots of high-fat foods. A burger bun, for example, is a good source of starchy carbohydrate, but the burger inside is likely to be very fatty! A wholemeal bread sandwich sounds like a healthy option but if the bread is very thin and the filling includes lots of cheese and mayonnaise (both of which contain fat), then it is no longer such a healthy choice.

Healthy hearts

Obesity is a term that is often used today. It refers to when a person is very overweight. Obesity is one of the causes of **coronary heart disease**. It also affects what type of activity a person is able to do.

The type of foods on offer today is part of the reason why there has been an increase in obesity and coronary heart disease. A lot of 'fast food' is high in fats and sugars and contains few complex carbohydrates. Food such as kebabs and burgers only fill you up for a short time so you feel hungry and need to eat again fairly soon.

Lack of exercise

As well as high fat meals, people do not exercise as much as they used to. Fewer young people walk to school because many households have a car and they spend more of their leisure time doing activities that do not require much energy, such as playing computer games. In addition to eating a healthy diet it is important to look after your body by taking regular exercise and getting plenty of fresh air.

Many people are overweight because they eat too many calories. The high fat content of many meals contributes to this because fat is higher in calories than protein and carbohydrate. Fat is also easily transferred into the fat cells compared with the other nutrients that have to break down first.

Staying healthy

You will have read a lot so far about the importance of the energy supplied by starchy carbohydrate foods. However, they have many other health benefits too. Complex carbohydrates, such as those in wholegrain foods, beans, vegetables, and fruit, can help reduce the risk of problems with the digestive system. This is because foods containing fibre help waste products travel through the digestive system (see pages 14 and 15). If there are no complex carbohydrates in the diet, the waste is not able to absorb moisture and becomes hard and dry. This makes it much more difficult for the waste to leave the body, leading to problems such as constipation.

Toilet trouble

Constipation is when someone has trouble going to the toilet. The waste matter (known as faeces or stools) is hard and does not travel easily through the digestive system. Sometimes this causes straining while on the toilet, which can then lead to **piles**. Another condition that can affect the digestive system is diverticular disease. This happens when pockets appear in the lining of the large intestine (also known as the colon), into which waste material gets trapped. Eating complex carbohydrates may also help reduce the risk of getting bowel cancer later in life.

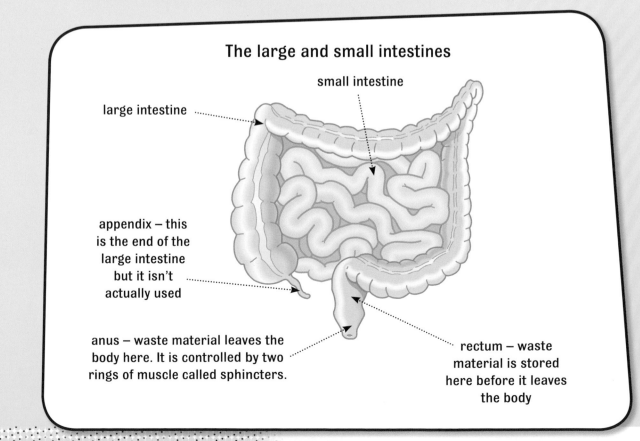

The large and small intestines

small intestine

large intestine

appendix – this is the end of the large intestine but it isn't actually used

anus – waste material leaves the body here. It is controlled by two rings of muscle called sphincters.

rectum – waste material is stored here before it leaves the body

Eating a balanced diet is the best way to stay healthy.

Healthy carbohydrates

Following a diet that contains plenty of "healthy" carbohydrates can also help reduce the chance of having appendicitis, which is what happens when the appendix becomes inflamed. Again, this is because waste material that is too dry becomes trapped in the appendix.

Not eating enough

Not eating enough food for a long time can be as harmful as eating too much. Your body needs a healthy balanced diet so that you can grow, repair your body, and do all the activities you want to do. Some people in **developing countries** do not always get enough food and may suffer diseases due to a lack of nutrients. Even in the Western world where there should be enough food for everyone, people sometimes suffer because they are not eating the right things. If people do not have much money they may buy cheap foods that are filling, such as chips, and eat these every day. Chips provide energy in the form of carbohydrates and fats, but they do not provide much of the other nutrients. If somebody eats a diet low in nutrients for a long time they will become ill and their body will not grow properly.

Labelling sugar

Today people are being encouraged to try to reduce the amount of sugar they eat. This includes the sugar that is added to drinks or used in food preparation. The natural sugars found in fruits and some vegetables are not seen as a health problem.

It contains what?

Many of today's ready-made meals and processed foods have to have extra ingredients added to them. It would not be possible to follow a cookery book recipe for apple pie and then expect it to stay fresh in the shops for a week. Products such as chocolate ice cream bars would not work unless extra ingredients were added. Sometimes **additives** are used to make foods last longer (preservatives) or to stop ingredients separating out (stabilizers).

Food fact

The ingredients listed below are from a chocolate ice cream bar containing caramel and nuts. They show that both sugar and glucose syrup are present in the caramel and in the ice cream.

You may be surprised by the foods that have sugar added.

Ingredients: Concentrated skimmed milk, milk chocolate (25%), caramel (8%) (concentrated skimmed milk, glucose syrup, sugar, vegetable fat, butteroil, stabiliser E410), sugar, glucose syrup, vegetable fat, whey solids; wheat crispies, (1%) (wheat flour, salt, raising agent E503), peanuts (1%), stabilizers, emulsifier, flavouring, colour.

INGREDIENTS:
Tomatoes (126g per 100g Ketchup)
Spirit Vinegar, Glucose Syrup, Sugar
Salt, Spice and Herb Extracts, Spice
Garlic Powder
SUITABLE FOR A GLUTEN FREE DIET
2mg Lycopene per 10ml serving

Sugars are often added to food products, particularly those that have reduced fat. Sugar can help to make foods tasty and give foods "body". However, it is not always possible to tell how much sugar is in a product just by reading the ingredients list.

All food products must be labelled to show their ingredients. Sugars are often listed under their chemical names rather than just saying "sugar". For example, the following are all names of sugars: sucrose, glucose, lactose, fructose, invert sugar, syrup, molasses, honey, and glucose syrup. This is why consumers do not always know exactly what they are eating or just how much sugar is contained in a product.

Sweet enough?

Many foods have added sweetness without the addition of sugar. Artificial sweeteners have been around for many years and they have the advantage of adding sweetness without adding energy (kJ). Non-sugar sweeteners are particularly useful for people with **diabetes** who must be careful about the amount of sugar in their diet.

Many people use artificial sweeteners to avoid the calories in sugar or because they have to limit the sugar in their diet.

Food labels

The way food products are labelled, and the information put on the label, is carefully controlled by law. It is important that people are not misled by a food label, particularly someone who has an **allergy** to an ingredient. You will find out more about food allergies on page 34.

Food products must, by law, show the following information:

- a name
- a list of ingredients, starting with the heaviest and ending with the lightest
- a label to show shelf-life, such as 'best before' or 'use by'
- any special storage conditions or conditions of use
- the manufacturer
- where the food came from
- instructions for use
- weight or volume of the contents (unless it weighs less than 5 grams)
- warnings about possible problems for allergy sufferers.

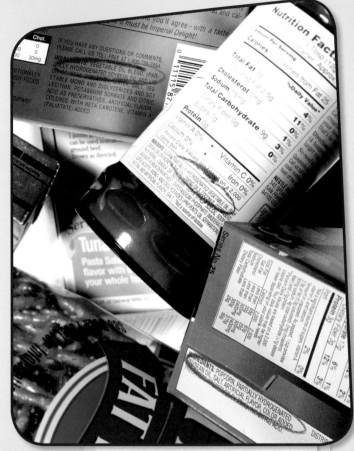

Packaged food must be accurately labelled so that consumers know exactly what they are buying.

Food fact

Use by dates are used for foods that go off quickly and may be unsafe to eat after this date. These dates are found on foods like fresh meat, fish, and cheese.

Best before dates are usually found on foods that will keep longer than a few days. They will not be at their best after this date. These dates are found on breakfast cereals, biscuits, and tinned foods.

What's in a name?

All packaged food must have a name that tells people exactly what is in the package. For example, the label could not say just "flour" because there are lots of different types of flour. It might say "wholemeal self-raising flour" or "white plain flour". The label must also say whether the food has been processed. This means that a packet of pasta might have a label saying "fresh" or "dried" depending how it has been made.

Reading labels

You can also find different starches listed in ingredients lists. These are starches that have been used in food production. For example, starches such as cornflour can thicken sauces. Thickeners or thickening agents are often used in reduced-sugar or low-sugar products. Sugar usually makes things set (like jam for example). When less sugar is used something else is needed to act as a **gelling agent**. Maize starch (from sweetcorn) and potato starch are commonly used as thickeners and may be seen on many food labels.

Starch is needed to thicken food products, such as this white sauce being used to top lasagne. Different starches can be seen listed on food labels.

Sugar control

Glucose is your body's main source of energy. The way your body uses glucose is controlled by several chemicals called **hormones**. One of these hormones is insulin. Unfortunately for some people their bodies are not able to produce enough insulin. This means their bodies cannot control their blood sugar level. The amount of glucose travelling around in their blood can become very high or very low. The result is a disease called diabetes mellitus.

Diabetes mellitus

A very high or very low level of glucose in the blood is serious. The levels must be controlled. Diabetes mellitus can be controlled by either modifying the diet or by taking tablets and/or insulin. Some diabetics need a daily injection of insulin while others need only be careful about what they eat. A diet high in complex carbohydrates and fibre (including wholemeal bread, wholegrain rice and cereals, vegetables, and fruit) is recommended because these foods help to control the rate at which sugar is absorbed into the blood.

Sweet treats

Someone with diabetes must make sure they do not have too much sugar or sugary foods and drinks, such as sweets, cakes, biscuits, or fizzy drinks. Sugary products will cause a sudden rise in blood sugar levels. However, they do not have to avoid sweet foods altogether. They can eat sweet treats occasionally, but it is better to eat them after a meal rather than on an empty stomach.

Young and old

It is not clear why people with diabetes do not make enough insulin in their bodies. There are two types of diabetes: type 1 (insulin dependent) and type 2 (non-insulin dependent). The first type usually develops suddenly with severe symptoms and normally happens before the age of forty.

Type 2 diabetes does not require treatment with insulin because some insulin is still produced in the body. This type of diabetes can be controlled by eating healthily or sometimes by tablets. This type tends to affect middle-aged and older people, although anyone who is overweight is at a higher risk of developing the disease as they get older.

FRANK'S STORY

Frank Reakes is 13 years old and was diagnosed with diabetes 10 months ago. Frank says: "Before I was diagnosed I noticed something was wrong; at school I couldn't concentrate and frequently asked to go to the toilet and get water. At home I was never hungry and I especially went to the toilet at night."

Having diabetes hasn't affected his lifestyle very much because he is still able to enjoy playing sport. However, he now has to avoid puddings and snacks. He also eats lots of complex carbohydrates like rice and pasta.

Having diabetes can affect the types of food you can eat, but you can still enjoy a wide variety of sports.

Food allergies

A food allergy is a reaction caused by eating a specific food or foods. Common foods most likely to cause an allergic reaction are milk, eggs, fish, shellfish, nuts, and soya beans. Gluten is found in wheat, which is used to make flour, a carbohydrate food. Coeliac disease is the name for an intolerance to gluten.

Gluten

Gluten is a protein found mainly in wheat, although it is also present in rye, barley, and oats. People with coeliac disease have a condition in which the walls of their small intestine become damaged if they eat gluten. When the villi (see page 16) in the lining of the small intestine are damaged, nutrients are not absorbed properly. The symptoms include stomach pain, sickness, tiredness, bloating, diarrhoea, and loss of weight.

Avoiding foods

Obviously someone with this allergy must avoid all foods containing gluten. Unfortunately this includes a huge range of foods because wheat is used to make flour. Just think how many products are made from flour: biscuits, cakes, most breads, pancakes, many sauces, pastries.

Anyone with coeliac disease must avoid foods like these, as they all contain gluten.

Lots of processed foods like desserts, snacks, and ready-made meals include starch-based thickeners containing gluten, so these must be avoided, too. Also, anything containing rye or barley may cause a reaction, as well as foods made using oats, such as porridge and flapjacks.

Coeliac specials

Fortunately many supermarkets now cater for coeliacs and provide a range of gluten-free products. Many foods have gluten-free labels to show they are safe for coeliacs to eat. Health food shops have sold products, such as bread and cakes, for coeliacs for some time.

Food fact

Someone with coeliac disease will need to avoid some or all of the following: barley, bran, cereal filler, malt, modified starch, oats, rusk, rye, semolina, starch, wheat flour. This means they must read food labels very carefully.

Some foods are labelled "gluten-free".

Staple starches

A staple food is the main food of a diet and is usually a food that provides energy. Starchy carbohydrate foods are called staple foods because they form a major part of the diet. Different countries and cultures have their own staples depending on their climate and what they are able to grow. One of Britain's staple foods is wheat because the weather is suitable for growing it – wheat doesn't need lots of sunshine! So the diet of most British people is based on what could be made with wheat, or the flour made from wheat. Bread used to be an important filler (food that fills you up) that was fairly cheap for people to buy.

Potty about potatoes

Potatoes are also regarded as one of Britain's staple foods. Many traditional dishes are based on potatoes, such as Shepherd's Pie, Cottage Pie, sausages and mash, and potato cakes. Even today many people would not consider a meal complete unless it was served with potatoes.

Lots of choice

Today you do not have to rely only on foods that can be grown and produced in this country. There are now many ways to preserve food so that it will keep longer including while it is transported from another country. This means you have a much wider choice of foods on offer. If you want bread you can now choose between ciabatta (from Italy), croissant (from France), rye bread (from Germany), or naan bread (from India). It is also now possible to make these products in the UK, so you may see croissants labelled "made in the UK".

Today we have a huge variety of breads to choose from.

Pass the pasta

Pasta is traditionally a staple food of Italy. It can now be bought fresh or dry or as part of a ready-made meal. Pasta is made with flour and sometimes eggs are added. The flour used for making pasta comes from durum wheat. This produces semolina flour, which is fine, gritty, and yellow in colour. Once the pasta dough has been made, it is cut, pressed, and moulded into different shapes and sizes.

Pasta parties

Pasta is a very healthy food. It is low in fats and high in complex carbohydrates. It even has a "high fibre" version – brown pasta provides more fibre.

Pasta comes in a huge range of shapes, sizes, and colours!

Worldwide diets

Rice is a staple food of several countries including India, China, and Japan. Like pasta, rice is low in fat and high in complex carbohydrates. Brown rice contains bran so it also provides fibre and has slightly more protein, iron, calcium, and B vitamins.

Rice dishes

There are many different varieties of rice so it is not surprising that there are also many different ways of cooking and serving it. Traditionally, in Britain, short grain pudding rice was soaked in milk and cooked slowly in the oven to make a rice pudding. In India, long grain rice is cooked in stock (flavoured liquid) with meat, fish, and/or vegetables to make a pilau. Japanese and Chinese dishes tend to use soft, sticky rice that can be shaped with the fingers (as in sushi) or picked up with chopsticks. The Italians are famous for risotto. Ladles of stock are slowly added to the risotto rice until it becomes creamy, plump, and tender.

Food fact

Long grain rice is about four to five times longer than it is wide. Examples include Basmati rice and Carolina rice.

Short grain rice has short, plump grains that tend to remain moist and cling together when cooked. Examples include Arborio (risotto) rice and pudding rice.

Cornmeal made from maize can be used to make polenta and cornbread.

Gluten free

Rice is also similar to pasta because it is a "slow-release" carbohydrate so it is a much better source of energy than the "instant" energy provided by sugary foods. In addition, rice is suitable for people with coeliac disease because it does not contain any gluten.

Puffed rice

Rice is not only eaten as grain in savoury and sweet dishes, but it can also be processed to make many other products. Grains of rice can be ground up to turn them into rice flour, ground rice, and flaked rice. These ingredients are then used to make puddings, cakes, biscuits, and as thickening agents for soups or stews. Rice can also be "puffed" to make puffed rice cereals and rice cake snacks.

 Couscous can be used as an alternative to rice.

Moroccan couscous

Couscous is the name of a tiny grain made from finely ground semolina wheat. It cooks very quickly in hot water or by being steamed. Today you can buy packets of dried couscous, some of which have flavours already added to them. Couscous is also the name of a spicy Moroccan dish that is served on a bed of couscous. Traditionally couscous was a staple food of North Africa.

Maize or corn?

Maize (also called corn) is a staple food of many countries including Italy, Mexico, and the United States. It can be used to make a wide range of products, such as tortillas (thin pancakes), polenta (a dough made from maize flour), breakfast cereals, cornbread, and even popcorn!

Eating for health

It is now known that the diet you eat throughout your life can affect your risk of getting diseases such as coronary heart disease. **Dietary guidelines** have been produced to help people choose a diet that contains foods needed for good health. These guidelines do not tell people *what* to eat but suggest different ways to follow a healthy diet. Dietary guidelines are produced by various health organizations, including governments.

Varied diet

Eating a variety of foods is important. People sometimes end up eating the same foods every day out of habit, laziness, or just because they like them. But in the long term this can lead to a lack of some nutrients and could cause health problems. There is not one single food that contains all the nutrients in the right quantities, which is why everyone should eat a variety of foods. When you think about the thousands of foods available it must be possible to find different ones that you like to eat.

Food fact

In the UK, the Food Standards Agency say the key to a healthy diet is to eat a variety of foods. For most people this means eating:

- more fruit and vegetables – eat lots! You can choose from fresh, frozen, tinned, dried, or juiced.
- more bread, cereals, and potatoes – these should make up about a third of your diet.
- less fat and sugar – try to eat fewer fatty or sugary foods.

 Drinking plenty of water is also part of a healthy diet.

The eatwell plate

The eatwell plate was produced to help people understand how to eat healthily. It is used by dieticians, health professionals, manufacturers, caterers, and in schools. However, it is not recommended for very young children or some people under medical supervision. The eatwell plate clearly shows the sort of foods that can be included in a healthy diet and in what proportion. For example, the section containing foods providing carbohydrate is quite big, while the section showing fatty and sugary foods is much smaller.

The eatwell plate shows the proportions of different foods that make up a healthy diet.

fruit and vegetables

bread, rice, potatoes, and pasta

meat, fish, eggs, and beans

fatty and sugary foods

milk and dairy foods

Achieving a balance

Eating a healthy diet is not just about the foods you choose. It is also about the way those foods are prepared and cooked. Potatoes are high in complex carbohydrate and provide vitamin C. But if potatoes are cut into thin slices and deep-fried, they will also contain lots of fat. Or, if the potatoes are boiled then left to go cold and reheated, any vitamin C present is likely to be lost. This is because vitamin C dissolves into the cooking water and is destroyed by heat. So, it is important to consider how foods are cooked.

Thick chips

Eating a healthy balanced diet does not mean you have to give up foods you enjoy. It just means you shouldn't eat them all the time. Eating chips occasionally is fine and it is even better if you can choose thick chips! If a potato is cut into "thick chips" rather than thin ones, it will absorb less fat when cooked.

Lots of foods can be just as tasty if they are cooked without using or adding fat. Eggs are a good example. They can be boiled, poached, or scrambled. Bacon is best grilled because the fat can drip into the grill pan so you do not have to eat it. Some foods can be "dry fried", which means no extra fat is added to the pan. There are some good non-stick frying pans that make this method possible.

» Potatoes can be eaten in a variety of ways; as long as you don't always eat fatty chips you can enjoy a healthy variety.

Saving vitamins

Vegetables are often cooked by boiling them in water. Some vitamins dissolve into the water during cooking and are lost when the vegetables are drained. It is better to steam or microwave vegetables as less water is needed and more of the vitamins are saved.

A healthy balanced diet should be part of everyone's lifestyle.

Carbohydrate in a variety of foods, broken down into starch, sugars, and fibre			
Food	Starches (grams)	Sugars (grams)	Fibre (grams)
1 small banana	2.3	20.9	1.1
1 small can baked beans	24	4	11
100 grams cauliflower	0.2	2.5	1.6
2 slices bread, brown	41.3	4	4
2 slices bread, white	43.8	2	2
100 grams flour, wheat, white, plain	76.2	1.5	3.6
100 grams flour, chapatti, white	75.6	2.1	4.1
100 grams golden syrup	0	79.0	0

Glossary

acid   something that tastes sour, for example vinegar or lemon juice

additive   substance (natural or artificial) added to foods to increase their shelf-life or to improve their colour, flavour, or texture

allergy   bad reaction caused by eating a particular food. Some people can become very ill from food allergies.

amino acids   building blocks of proteins. Different amino acids combine together to form a protein.

bacteria   micro-organisms (living things) that are so small they can only be seen through a microscope. Some are helpful, such as those in our intestines, and some can be harmful, such as those that cause food poisoning.

basal metabolic rate (BMR)   rate at which your body burns food when it is completely rested

blood sugar level   amount of glucose in the blood. This will rise after sugar has been eaten and will gradually fall until food is eaten again.

bran   outer layer of a grain of wheat

calorie   measurement of energy supplied by food

carbon dioxide   gas present in our breath when we breathe out

cells   microscopic living things that make up all living matter

chemical reaction   something that occurs between two or more chemicals

cholesterol   fatty substances found in the body

chyme   mushy liquid that passes from the stomach to the small intestine. It is formed from partly digested food mixed with the digestive juices of the stomach.

complex carbohydrates   carbohydrates that cannot be broken down by the human digestive system, such as the bran in wholemeal bread

coronary heart disease   illness that affects the heart. When the vessels leading to the heart become blocked by fatty substances the blood cannot get to the heart as easily.

developing countries   less developed countries are often poorer and do not have well established industries and services, such as transport, schools, or welfare

diabetes   when the body does not have enough insulin (a hormone) to control the amount of glucose in the blood

dietary guidelines   suggestions for healthy eating

dietician   person who advises people about what they should eat

digest   process of breaking down food when it is eaten. Digestion starts in the mouth when you bite and chew food and continues until the molecules that make up food are taken into the bloodstream.

digestive juices   liquids containing enzymes that help to break down food during digestion. Saliva and gastric juices are examples of digestive juices.

digestive system   all the parts of the body that are used to digest food

dissolve   to gradually disappear in a liquid

duodenum   first part of the small intestine

energy   what the body needs to stay alive. Energy is supplied by foods.

enzyme   something that helps a chemical reaction to take place faster without being changed itself

fats   nutrients in a wide range of foods, especially fatty ones

fatty acids   small units that fat is broken down into during digestion

fibre   name for the parts of a carbohydrate that your body cannot break down. It is found in wholewheat foods, bran, the skin of fruits and vegetables, and baked beans.

fluoride   mineral often added to toothpaste to help build strong teeth

gelling agent   something that helps a food product set, and gives it shape and structure

germ   part of the wheat grain. It contains some of the vitamins and fats.

glucose   smallest unit that carbohydrates can be broken down into during digestion

glycogen   name for any glucose stored in the liver and muscles following absorption. Extra glucose is stored if it is not needed immediately by the body.

hormones   substances produced by different glands in the body that affect or control particular organs, cells, or tissues

ileum   third and last part of the small intestine

insoluble fibre   type of fibre that will not dissolve

jejunum   middle part of the small intestine

kilojoules (kJ)   measurement of energy supplied by food

large intestine   part of the intestines through which undigested food passes after it has left the small intestine

liver   organ in the body used in the digestive system

marathon   long-distance running race

mead   fermented drink made out of honey

minerals   nutrients needed by the body in small amounts

molecules   very small parts of a substance

natural sugars   sugars naturally present in food, not added

nervous system   series of connected nerves throughout the body

nutrients   carbohydrates, proteins, fats, vitamins, and minerals are all nutrients. Foods and most drinks contain different amounts and types of nutrients.

nutritionist   person who studies nutrients and how the body uses them

obesity   state of being extremely overweight

oesophagus   tube through which food travels from the mouth to the stomach

organ   internal body part, such as the liver, stomach, or intestines

oxygen   gas present in the air and used by the body when we breathe in

piles   collection of swollen veins around the anus caused by a diet low in fibre, which leads to straining

preserve   to protect food from going "off". Food can be preserved for a short time by cooking it or putting it in the fridge. It can be preserved for longer by freezing, canning, bottling, vacuum packing, jamming, irradiating, drying, pickling, or adding preservatives.

processed   describes foods that have been changed to make them easier to prepare, cook and/or eat

proteins   nutrients supplied by foods such as meat, fish, and nuts

small intestine   part of the intestine into which food passes from the stomach to be digested and then absorbed into the blood. Undigested food passes right through the small intestine into the large intestine.

soluble fibre   fibre that can be dissolved

villi   tiny bumps in the intestines through which digested food and water is absorbed

vitamins   nutrients needed by the body in small amounts

wholemeal   food that uses the whole of the wheat grain

Find out more

Books

Making Healthy Food Choices: Special Diets and Food Allergies, Carol Ballard (Heinemann Library, 2006)
Our Bodies: Digestion, Steve Parker (Wayland, 2005)

Websites

www.bbc.co.uk/health/healthy_living/nutrition
This site provides lots of information about different foods, dietary requirements, and the needs of people at various stages of life.

www.coeliac.co.uk/
Provides information about coeliac disease.

www.diabetes.org.uk
Provides information and leaflets about diabetes.

www.eatwell.gov.uk
This site provides the latest news from the Government's Food Standards Agency relating to food and health. Topics include healthy diet, keeping food safe, food labels, and health issues.

www.fabflour.co.uk
Provides information and resources about wheat and flour.

www.foodstandards.gov.uk
This is the Government's information website for the Food Standards Agency.

www.potato.org.uk
Provides information about potatoes as well as recipes.

Contacts

Diabetes UK Central Office
Macleod House
10 Parkway
London NW1 7AA
Tel: 020 7424 1000

Eating Disorders Association
First Floor, Wensum House
103 Prince of Wales Road
Norwich
Norfolk NR1 1DW
Youth Helpline 0845 634 7650
http://www.b-eat.co.uk/Home

Coeliac UK
Suites A–D Octagon Court
High Wycombe
Bucks HP11 2HS
Tel: 01494 437278
http://coeliac.org.uk/13.asp

The Flour Advisory Bureau Ltd
21 Arlington Street
London
SW1A 1RN
Tel: 020 7493 2521

Index

absorption 16–17
additives 28
amino acids 17
appendicitis 27
artificial sweeteners 29

basal metabolic rate (BMR) 20
blood sugar levels 19, 32
bloodstream 6, 14, 16, 17, 18
bran 10, 38
bread 4, 7, 9, 10, 25, 32, 36, 40

calories 12, 13
cancer 26
carbohydrates
    complex carbohydrates 7, 10, 19, 23,
    25, 26, 32, 37, 38, 42
    health benefits 5, 26
    simple carbohydrates 6
carbon dioxide 18
coeliac disease 34–35, 39
constipation 26
cooking methods 13, 42–43
couscous 6, 39

diabetes 29, 32–33
dietary guidelines 40
digestion 6, 7, 10, 14–15, 16, 26
diverticular disease 26

eatwell plate 41
energy 4, 5, 7, 12, 13, 14, 18, 19, 24,
    26, 32, 39
energy release 18, 19, 21
energy requirements 20, 21
energy values 12, 13
enzymes 14
exercise 20, 21, 25

fast foods 24, 25
fats 4, 5, 13, 16, 20, 21, 22, 25, 29, 32, 42
fatty acids 17
fibre 6, 7, 10–11, 15, 17, 26, 32, 37, 38, 43
food allergies 30, 34–35
food labelling 28–31
fructose 22, 23, 29

glucose 6, 9, 12, 15, 17, 18, 19, 21, 22,
    28, 29, 32
gluten 34, 35, 39
glycogen 12, 15, 18, 21

healthy diet 20, 25, 26, 40, 42
heart disease 25, 40

insulin 32, 33

kilojoules (kJ) 12, 13, 20

liver 12, 15, 17, 18

nutrients 4, 5, 10, 16, 23, 26, 34, 40

obesity 25
oxygen 18

pasta 4, 6, 7, 9, 21, 37
piles 26
potatoes 4, 6, 9, 13, 36, 40, 42
preserved foods 8, 36
processed foods 10, 28, 31, 35, 39
proteins 4, 5, 13, 16, 21, 34, 38

rice 4, 6, 7, 9, 38–39

saliva 9, 14, 22
small intestine 14, 15, 16
snack foods 33
staple foods 36–39
starches 6, 9, 31, 35, 36, 43
sugars 4, 6, 8, 12, 22, 23, 25, 28, 29,
    31, 32, 43
sweets 19, 22, 23, 32

tooth decay 22

villi 16, 34
vitamins and minerals 5, 11, 23, 38, 42, 43

waste products 10, 15, 17, 26, 27
water 4, 5, 13, 15, 17, 19
weight loss 20
wheat 10, 34, 35, 36
wholemeal products 7, 10, 25, 32

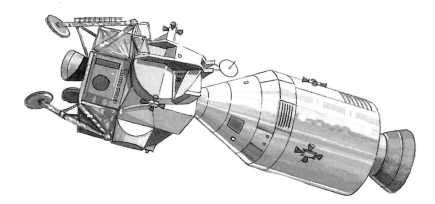

26999

Author:

Ian Graham was born in Belfast in 1953. He
studied applied physics at City University,
London, and took a postgraduate diploma in
journalism at the same university, specialising in
science and technology. He has written more than
one hundred children's non-fiction books and
numerous magazine articles.

Artist:

David Antram was born in Brighton, England,
in 1958. He studied at Eastbourne College of Art
and then worked in advertising for fifteen years
before becoming a full-time artist. He has
illustrated many children's non-fiction books.

Series creator:

David Salariya was born in Dundee,
Scotland. He has illustrated a wide range of books
and has created and designed many new series for
publishers both in the UK and overseas. In 1989,
he established The Salariya Book Company. He
lives in Brighton with his wife, illustrator Shirley
Willis, and their son Jonathan.

Editor:

Karen Barker Smith

Published in Great Britain in 2003 by
Book House, an imprint of
The Salariya Book Company Ltd
25 Marlborough Place, Brighton BN1 1UB

Please visit the Salariya Book Company at:
www.salariya.com
www.book-house.co.uk

ISBN 1 904194 55 9

A catalogue record for this book is available
from the British Library.

Printed and bound in China.
Printed on paper from sustainable forests.

Avoid being on Apollo 13!

I'm sure 13 is an unlucky number!

Written by
Ian Graham

Illustrated by
David Antram

Created and designed by
David Salariya

The Danger Zone

BOOK HOUSE

Contents

Introduction   5

Practice makes perfect   6

The Apollo spacecraft   8

Launch day   10

Liftoff!   12

Goodbye Earth   14

Living in a tin can   16

Houston, we've had a problem   18

Failure is not an option   20

Cold, wet and stuffy   22

Lost mission   24

Going home   26

Down to Earth   28

Glossary   30

Index   32

Introduction

It is April 1970. You are an American astronaut about to climb into a spacecraft and fly to the moon. You have been training for years for the chance to take part in this mission. You watched two members of the Apollo 11 crew, Neil Armstrong and Buzz Aldrin, become the first people ever to walk on another world. They landed on the moon in July 1969. They were followed by Charles Conrad and Alan Bean of the Apollo 12 mission in November that year. The whole world watched them explore the moon on television.

Now it is your turn. You are a member of the three-man crew of Apollo 13. Some people think that 13 is an unlucky number – you don't know it yet, but Apollo 13 will be an incredibly unlucky mission. On your way to the moon, your spacecraft will suffer the most serious accident to happen during a moon-landing mission. It is so serious that no one knows if you will be able to get back to Earth. Your fate depends on hundreds of engineers on Earth working out how to get you home safely. You wouldn't want to be on Apollo 13!

Practice makes perfect

The whole crew practices everything that you will have to do during the mission. You do it over and over again until you could do it in your sleep. You train in simulators that look exactly like the real spacecraft. The mission controllers keep you on your toes by surprising you with all sorts of emergencies to see how well you deal with them. If you're going to make a mistake, it is better to do it in the simulator than on the way to the moon. By the time launch day comes, you have to know the spacecraft inside out, be able to fly it perfectly and know what to do in any situation.

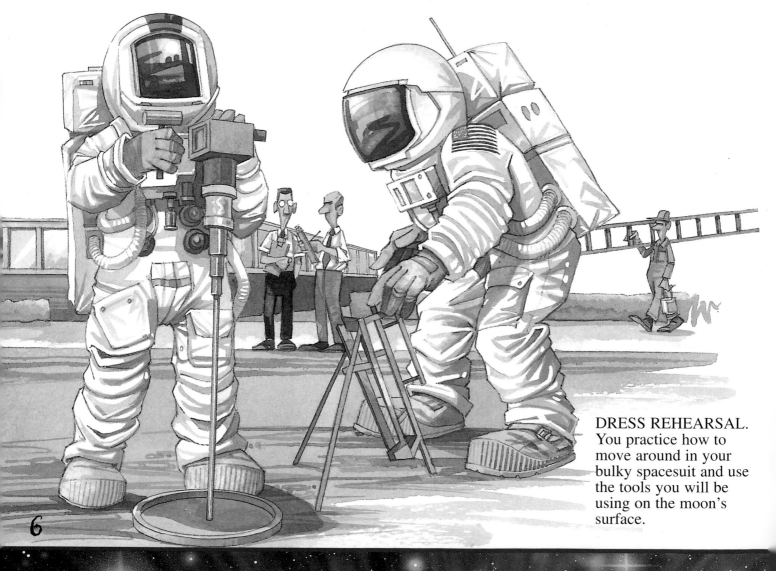

DRESS REHEARSAL. You practice how to move around in your bulky spacesuit and use the tools you will be using on the moon's surface.

Handy hint

Remember to lock your spacesuit helmet firmly in place before you're lowered into the water tank for a training session!

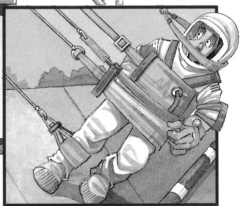

FLYING SPIDER. You practise flying a spider-like jet-craft designed to fly exactly like the Apollo Lunar Module.

WEIGHTLESSNESS is simulated in a training aeroplane (left). So many people get airsick in this plane that it's nicknamed the 'Vomit Comet'!

ON THE MOON, you will weigh one sixth as much as you weigh on Earth because the moon has less gravity. You're hung sideways so that you can see what it's like to weigh so little (right).

UNDERWATER. You practice making spacewalks in a huge water tank (left). The uplift you get from the water provides the closest thing to weightlessness on Earth.

BUG ALERT! Someone the crew works with catches German measles. To avoid becoming ill in space, one crew member with no immunity to it is replaced two days before launch.

7

The Apollo spacecraft

The week before the launch, you visit the giant Vehicle Assembly Building at Cape Canaveral, Florida, to watch the Apollo spacecraft being hoisted on top of its rocket. The spacecraft is made of three parts, or modules: the Command Module, the Service Module and the Lunar Module. Every Apollo crew gives its Command and Lunar Modules names. For Apollo 13, the Command Module is called *Odyssey* and the Lunar Module is called *Aquarius*.

The Saturn V is the biggest rocket ever to launch people into space. It is actually three rockets, called stages, standing on top of each other. As each stage uses up its fuel, it falls away and the next stage takes over.

GIANT LAUNCHER. The huge Saturn V rocket stands 111 metres from the base of its first-stage engines to the tip of the Apollo spacecraft at the top. It will be launched 13 times and is successful every time.

Saturn V rocket

Launch escape system

Boost protective cover

111 metres

I'm glad it won't be me sitting at the top of this thing!

Heat shield

Docking probe

Head pad

Handy hint

Watch out! Don't ever get in the way of the crawler transporter when it is on the move. This massive vehicle doesn't stop for anyone!

Crew couches

LAUNCH PAD. The rocket and spacecraft sitting on their mobile launch platform weighs 4,800 tonnes. This is slowly carried out to the launch pad by the world's biggest transport vehicle.

Command Module

HOME FROM HOME. You will travel to the moon inside the tiny Command Module. It is the only part of the Apollo spacecraft that will return to Earth. It measures only 3.2 m high and 3.9 m wide. For most of the journey, it is connected to the Service Module. The Service Module contains fuel, oxygen and the rocket engine that blasts the craft back from the moon to Earth. The Lunar Module is designed to land two astronauts on the moon.

Service Module

Crawler transporter

Adaptor

Lunar Module

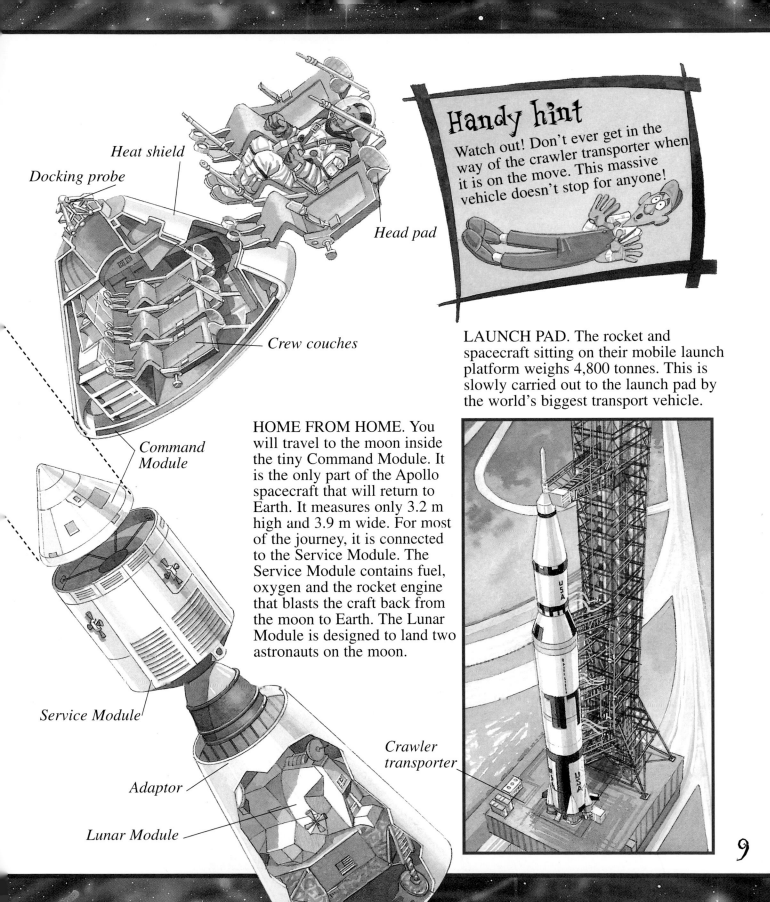

9

Launch day

Countdown to takeoff

WAKEY, WAKEY! You are called precisely four hours and 17 minutes before launch.

SAY 99. The flight doctor gives you a final once-over four hours and two minutes before launch to make sure you are in top condition.

Launch day has arrived. It is 11th April 1970. Your 400,000-kilometre journey to the moon begins a few hours from now with a trip into orbit around the Earth. While you and the rest of the crew go through your preparations for takeoff, a team of engineers gets the spacecraft and its mighty rocket ready for you. You can't waste any time. Everything, from filling the rocket's fuel tanks to having your breakfast, has its own time slot in the carefully planned countdown. It's too late to change your mind now!

BREAKFAST. At 'eggs-actly' three hours and 32 minutes before launch, you have breakfast – steak, eggs, orange juice, coffee and toast – and then put on your spacesuit.

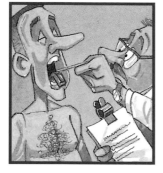

SNOOPY CAP. This soft cap (4) contains earpieces and a microphone for radio communications. A clear 'fishbowl' helmet (5) locks onto the top of the suit and gloves lock onto metal rings at the ends of the sleeves (6).

SUITING UP. The various parts of the spacesuit are put on in order. Electrodes (1) are glued to your chest to monitor your heartbeat. Underwear – a pair of 'long johns' (2) – is the first layer next to the skin. Next, you pull on the spacesuit legs, push your head through the neck ring and pull on the body and arms (3).

I'm suited up and ready to go!

Helmet

Mission badge

Watch

Boots

Handy hint
If you need to scratch your nose or sneeze, do it BEFORE your helmet is fitted! You can't take your helmet off again until you're in orbit.

ALL ABOARD. Precisely three hours and seven minutes before launch you board the crew transfer van. You arrive at launch pad 39A 12 minutes later.

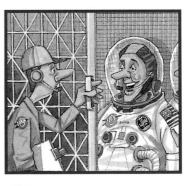

GOING UP. You take a lift to the top of the launch tower and walk across the access arm into the white room next to the Command Module. The white room team is waiting for you.

TAKE A SEAT. You board the spacecraft 2 hours and 40 minutes before launch. Take care not to snag your spacesuit as you slide through the hatch. Each one costs US$1.5 million!

11

Liftoff!

When the countdown reaches zero, you start a 12-minute rollercoaster ride through Earth's atmosphere to space. As the rocket leaves the launch pad, the time on the clock at Mission Control in Houston, Texas, is 13.13! Pictures of the soaring rocket and its flight path appear on a big display screen at Mission Control.

T (TAKEOFF) –3 MINUTES, 7 SECONDS. The Saturn V rocket is given the firing command that starts its automatic launch sequence. Computers start its fuel pumps.

T –8.9 SECONDS. The first-stage engines fire. The rocket is held down on the launch pad until all five engines are running.

ZERO. Apollo 13 and the 3,000-tonne Saturn V launch-rocket gently lift off the launch pad.

BROOARR

Apollo 13's bad luck first strikes when one of the rocket engines shuts down two minutes early. For a few moments, you don't know if Apollo 13 will make it into space. The remaining engines fire for longer to make up for the fault. Engineers at Mission Control check that there is enough fuel left to send the spacecraft to the moon.

Handy hint

Crash

Bounce

Make sure you are strapped tightly into your seat. If you aren't, you'll bounce around the Command Module like a cork in a bottle when the rocket blasts off!

T +3 MINUTES, 20 SECONDS. The launch escape tower's rockets fire, carrying the tower and boost protective cover away from the top of the spacecraft.

T +2 MINUTES, 44 SECONDS. The empty first stage falls away and 2 seconds later the second-stage engines fire.

T +9 MINUTES, 53 SECONDS. The empty second stage falls away. Three seconds later, the third-stage engines fire.

T +12 MINUTES, 39 SECONDS. The spacecraft is safely in orbit around Earth. Time to check that everything is working properly.

13

Goodbye Earth

The spacecraft checks out fine, so you get the go-ahead to fire the third-stage engine and head for the moon. The engine boosts your speed from 28,000 kilometres per hour (kph) to the 40,000 kph needed to break away from Earth's gravity. Once you are safely on your way to the moon, there is a very important job to do. The Lunar Module is packed away inside the top of the rocket, underneath the Command and Service Modules (CSM). The CSM has to be separated from the rocket and turned around so that it can pull the Lunar Module out. This delicate manoeuvre requires pinpoint flying. Nothing less will do.

STEADY AS YOU GO. Thrusters nudge the spacecraft slowly forwards and away from the end of Saturn V's third stage (above).

TURNAROUND. The thrusters are fired again to turn the spacecraft around. The end of the rocket opens up like a giant flower, revealing the Lunar Module (above).

STEERING. You steer the spacecraft by using hand controllers to fire rocket thrusters on the Service Module.

Piece of cake!

Handy hint

If you suffer from space sickness, grab a bag fast. Remember, during weightlessness EVERYTHING floats around the spacecraft – yuck!

Docking probe

DOCKING. The CSM eases forwards and docks with the Lunar Module (above). A probe on top of it fits into a hole on top of the Lunar Module and the two craft lock together.

EASY DOES IT. The CSM slowly backs up and pulls the Lunar Module out of the end of the rocket (above). It all goes perfectly. You are on your way.

15

Living in a tin can

Being an Apollo astronaut sometimes feels like living inside a tiny tin can. You have to get along with two other people in that small space for more than a week. You have to get used to noise all the time too. The spacecraft is never completely silent. There is the hum of air pumps, voices on the radio and the sounds of other crew-members moving about. The temperature is kept at a steady 22°C, so once you're in orbit, you can take off the bulky spacesuit you wore for the launch and put on a more comfortable flight suit. In orbit you experience weightlessness and can just float around inside the spacecraft.

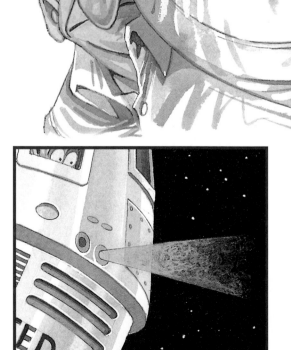

SPACE FOOD. You wish you could eat 'normal' food. Most space food is dried to save weight in the spacecraft (left). You add water to make it edible.

GOING TO THE TOILET. Three astronauts produce a lot of urine during a mission. To save weight, it is dumped overboard (right).

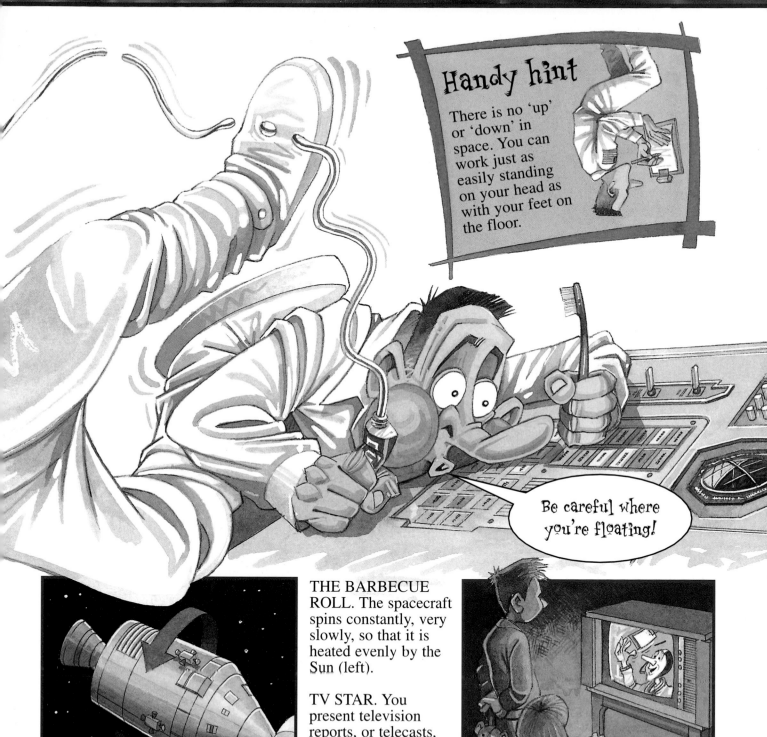

Handy hint

There is no 'up' or 'down' in space. You can work just as easily standing on your head as with your feet on the floor.

Be careful where you're floating!

THE BARBECUE ROLL. The spacecraft spins constantly, very slowly, so that it is heated evenly by the Sun (left).

TV STAR. You present television reports, or telecasts, from the spacecraft to show viewers how the flight is going (right).

17

Houston, we've had a problem

On 13th April, Apollo 13 is 329,000 km away from Earth. Each day the moon looks bigger through the Command Module windows. Mission Control asks you to turn on fans inside the Service Module's oxygen tanks. As soon as the switch is hit, you hear a loud bang. You watch your instruments in horror. The spacecraft seems to be losing oxygen and electrical power. You struggle to understand what has happened. Mission controllers on Earth can't believe what they see on their computer screens.

Disaster strikes

1. THE JOLT. You hear a bang and the spacecraft shakes violently. You think it might have been hit by a piece of space rock.

2. ALARMS go off in the spacecraft and at Mission Control. You watch your instruments in disbelief.

3. WHAT'S HAPPENING? Mission controllers think their computers have gone crazy. Their screens don't seem to make sense.

4. GAS ESCAPE. You look through a window and see something spraying out into space. It must be oxygen!

5. LOSING POWER. Your instruments show that the Command Module's fuel cells are losing power fast.

6. MOVE OUT! You quickly power down the Command Module and move into the Lunar Module so that you can use its air and electricity.

WHAT HAPPENED? Later, it is discovered that an electrical fault blew up an oxygen tank and damaged equipment in the Service Module.

19

Failure is not an option

At Mission Control, the flight director tells everyone to find a way to get the crew home. He shouts, "Failure is not an option!" Ground controllers and engineers immediately start discussing what to do.

Some of them want to turn the spacecraft around and bring it straight back to Earth. Others want to let the spacecraft keep going and use the moon's gravity to swing it round and back to Earth. This option would take longer. The long way would be less risky, but no one knows if the spacecraft's oxygen and electricity will last long enough. You keep calling Mission Control to ask for their decision, but they're still working out what to do for the best.

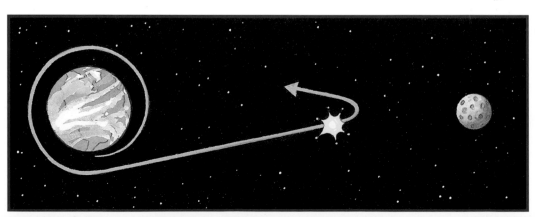

Option One

The spacecraft does a U-turn and comes straight home. It gets you home fast, but you would have to fire the Service Module engine. It might be damaged, it might not work and it might explode.

Handy hint

Watch your instruments like a hawk. They tell you exactly what is happening in the rest of the spacecraft, especially all the parts that you can't see.

Those are our options, gentlemen. Let's get those astronauts home safely.

Option two

Mission controllers decide it's safer to carry on to the moon and swing behind it. You can use the Lunar Module engine to stay on course, but it wasn't designed for this. Will this plan work?

21

Cold, wet and stuffy

Keeping warm is not as important as getting home alive, so the spacecraft heaters are switched off to save electricity. The temperature falls to just above freezing.

Moisture from your breath condenses on the cold instrument panels, walls and windows. The whole spacecraft is wet. It is dark too, because most of the lights are switched off. It gets very stuffy – the Lunar Module was designed for two astronauts, not three, so it can't purify the air fast enough. The breathed-out carbon dioxide in the air rises to a dangerous level. If it continues to rise, you will lose consciousness! You have to do something about it.

A bit of do-it-yourself

Fit this ← *into a hole made for this* →

THE COMMAND MODULE has air purifier canisters that could freshen the air, but they are square. The fittings in the Lunar Module are round. You make them fit by using pieces of hose, sticky tape, plastic bags and rubber bands (right). It works! The amount of carbon dioxide in the air starts falling.

A wee problem!

The crippled spacecraft is so hard to control that you have to stop dumping urine overboard. When it sprays out into space it pushes the spacecraft off course. So you have to save it all in plastic bags and store them inside the spacecraft!

shiver

22

Lost mission

If everything had gone as planned, Apollo 13 would have landed on part of the moon called Fra Mauro. Apollo 11 and 12 landed in the Sea of Tranquillity and the Ocean of Storms. The ground there was flat because lava had flowed over it. Scientists wanted samples of older rocks from the hills and mountains that hadn't been covered by lava, but these places are more dangerous to land. The earlier missions proved that astronauts could fly the Lunar Module manually and choose a safe landing spot. It was decided that *Aquarius* from Apollo 13 would land in the Fra Mauro hills.

SPACESUIT. The spacesuit you would have worn on the moon (right) has extra-tough gloves, boots and a visor over the helmet to keep your head cool. You would also have worn a backpack with oxygen and a radio.

If nothing had gone wrong...

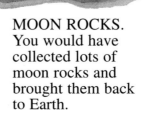

MOON ROCKS. You would have collected lots of moon rocks and brought them back to Earth.

HEAT FLOW. You would have drilled holes in the moon's surface to test how heat flows through it.

Handy hint

Be careful not to fall over on your back or you could be stranded there. You would not be able to get up because of the moon's low gravity.

What a fantastic view!

SOLAR WIND. You would have collected samples of the solar wind – particles that stream out of the Sun and hit the moon.

PHOTOGRAPHY. You would have taken thousands of close-up photographs of dust, rocks and craters on the moon's surface.

MOONQUAKES. You were planning to put instruments on the moon's surface to detect the vibrations of moonquakes.

LONE ORBITER. While two astronauts explored the surface, the third would orbit the moon alone in the Command Module.

25

Going home

Lunar Module

Command and Service Module (CSM)

You receive new instructions from Mission Control. You are to fire the Lunar Module's descent stage engine to change course. If it works it will send you around the moon and back to Earth. This engine was not designed to be used like this. It is the engine that would have slowed the Lunar Module down as it approached the moon's surface. The engine has to be fired before you reach the moon and again just after you reappear from behind it. While you are behind the moon, you are out of contact with Mission Control. If something goes wrong, no one can help you.

NERVOUS WAIT. As the spacecraft disappears behind the moon, everyone in Mission Control can only wait and hope that the burn (the firing of the engine) has gone well.

WHAT A VIEW! You gaze out of the Lunar Module's windows at the moon as you fly over your landing site at Fra Mauro. Then Earth slips out of sight as you fly behind the moon.

Handy hint

Remember to close the Command Module hatch before you undock the Lunar Module and cast it adrift. Otherwise you'll be sucked out into space!

That would've been a great place to visit.

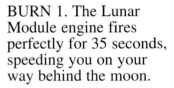

BURN 1. The Lunar Module engine fires perfectly for 35 seconds, speeding you on your way behind the moon.

FIRST SIGHT. When the Service Module is finally cast adrift, you gasp as you catch your first sight of the damage (left). The explosion has blown out one whole side, from top to bottom.

GOODBYE LUNAR MODULE. You power up the damp, cold and dark Command Module and prepare for your return to Earth. You cast the Lunar Module adrift (right) and say goodbye to the craft that acted as your lifeboat.

BURN 2. You fire the Lunar Module engine again for four minutes to speed up your return flight to Earth (above).

27

Down to Earth

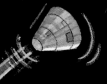

You are nearly home but you still face the most dangerous part of the mission – re-entering the Earth's atmosphere. It is very important to keep the spacecraft on course so that it hits the atmosphere at the right angle. If it comes in at the wrong angle it will either burn up or bounce off.

The heat shield glows red hot. It is all that stands between you and the extreme heat outside. No one knows if it was damaged by the explosion. The air around the spacecraft gets so hot that radio waves can't get through. You can't talk to Mission Control and they can't hear you. They do not know if you are alive or dead.

TOO SHALLOW. A spacecraft hitting Earth's atmosphere at too shallow an angle would bounce off it like a stone skipping across water.

TOO STEEP. If the Command Module dives into the atmosphere at too steep an angle, it will get too hot and burn up.

CHUTES OPEN. The Command Module falls through the clouds and floats down under three huge parachutes.

Handy hint

When you step out onto the deck of the recovery ship don't get too close to anyone – remember, you haven't had a bath for a whole week!

WELCOME HOME. You step out of the helicopter onto the deck of the recovery ship and wave to the crew and cameras.

"13 CALLING". Cheering breaks out at Mission Control as the radio crackles into life and you report in (above).

SPLASHDOWN. The module hits the ocean with a mighty splash (below left). You're safely back on Earth.

DIVERS KNOCK on the spacecraft hatch (below) and help you out to a waiting helicopter.

29

Glossary

Boost protective cover The cover that protected the Apollo Command Module during launch.

Burn A short firing of a rocket engine to change a spacecraft's course.

Canisters A container, usually made of metal.

Cape Canaveral A place in Florida, USA, where the John F. Kennedy Space Center is located. Many space flights are launched from there.

Carbon dioxide A gas that is breathed out by people.

Command Module The cone-shaped part of an Apollo spacecraft where the crew lived.

Crawler transporter The giant vehicle that moved Saturn V rockets from their assembly building to the launch pad.

CSM The Command and Service Module, a spacecraft made from the Command Module and Service Module linked together.

Fuel cell A device that uses oxygen and hydrogen gases to make electricity and water.

Gravity The force that pulls everything towards a large object such as a planet or moon.

Hatch A doorway in a spacecraft.

Heat shield The part of a spacecraft that protects the rest of the craft from the heat of re-entry.

Launch escape tower A rocket designed to fly the Command Module away to safety in an emergency during launch.

Lava Molten rock that flows out onto the surface of a planet or moon.

Lunar Module The part of an Apollo spacecraft designed to land on the moon.

Manually Done by hand instead of being done automatically by machines.

Mission Control The building where the space flights are monitored and managed.

Orbit To travel in a circle around a planet or moon.

Oxygen A gas humans need to breathe. It was also used to make water and electricity in the Apollo spacecraft.

Particle An extremely small piece or speck of something.

Recovery ship A ship sent to where a spacecraft is expected to land to pick up the crew.

Re-entry Coming back into the Earth's atmosphere from space.

Service Module The part of an Apollo spacecraft that supplied the Command Module with oxygen, water, electricity and rocket power.

Simulator A machine made to look like a vehicle, such as a spacecraft, used to train pilots.

Stage Part of a larger rocket with its own engine or engines, that falls away when its fuel is used up.

Thruster A small rocket engine used to adjust the position of a spacecraft while in space.

Index

A

access arm 11
air purifiers 22
Aldrin, Buzz 5
Aquarius 8, 24
Armstrong, Neil 5
astronaut 5, 8, 9, 16, 22, 25
atmosphere 10, 28, 31
automatic launch sequence 12

B

barbecue roll 17
Bean, Alan 5
boost protective cover 13, 30

C

Cape Canaveral 8, 30
carbon dioxide 22, 30
Command Module (CM) 8, 9, 11, 13, 14, 18, 19, 25-28, 30
Conrad, Charles 5
crawler transporter 9, 30
CSM (Command and Service Module) 14, 15, 30

F

flight director 20
flight suit 16
food 10, 16
Fra Mauro 24, 26
fuel 8-10, 13
fuel cells 19, 30

G

gravity 14, 20, 30

H

hand controllers 15
heat shield 9, 28, 30
helmet 7, 10, 11

I

illness 7

L

launch 10, 11, 16
launch escape tower 13, 31
launch pad 9, 11, 12
lava 24, 31
Lunar Module 7-9, 14, 15, 19, 21, 22, 24, 26, 27, 31

M

Mission Control 12, 13, 18, 20, 21, 26, 29, 31
mobile launch platform 9
moon 5-7, 9, 10, 13, 14, 18, 20, 21, 24-27
moonquakes 25
moon rocks 24

O

Odyssey 8
orbit 10, 11, 13, 16, 25, 31
oxygen 9, 18-20, 31

P

parachutes 29

R

recovery ship 29, 31
re-entry 28, 31
rocket 8-9, 10, 12-13, 14
rocket stage 8, 12, 13, 26

S

Saturn V 8, 12, 14
Service Module (SM) 8, 9, 14, 15, 18-20, 27, 31
simulator 6, 31
solar wind 25
space sickness 15
spacesuit 6, 7, 10, 11, 16, 24
splashdown 29
stage 8, 12, 13, 31

T

takeoff 10, 12
telecasts 17
temperature 16, 22
thrusters 14, 31
toilet 16
training 6-7

V

Vehicle Assembly Building 8
'Vomit Comet' 7

W

weightlessness 7, 16